The YO-YO Book

The YO-YO Book

By John E. Ten Eyck

Ilustrations by David Cain

Workman Publishing
New York

Special Thanks To:

Mark Brataas, Treasurer, AYYA
Dale Oliver, Oliver Toys
Lucky Meisenheimer, Yo-Yo Collector, AYYA
John Stangle, AYYA

Text copyright © 1998 Workman Publishing
Line illustrations copyright © 1998 David Cain
Front cover photography copyright © 1998 John Bean
Back cover photography (top) copyright © 1998 Lawrence Migdale
(For interior photography credits, please see p. 168.)

Library of Congress Cataloguing-in-Publication Data
Ten Eyck, John (John E.)
The Yo-Yo book/by John Ten Eyck; line drawings by David Cain.
p. cm.
Includes bibliographical references (p.)
ISBN 0-7611-0906-4
1. Yo-yos. I. Title.
GV1216.T46 1998
796.2—dc21   98-10180 CIP

Workman Publishing Company, Inc.
708 Broadway
New York, NY 10003-9555

Manufactured in the United States of America
First printing February 1998
10 9 8 7

Contents

Level 3 Tricks

Level 4 Tricks

Let's YO!

Introduction

If a yo-yo could talk, it would tell you its life isn't easy. Every minute of every day, a yo-yo is either all wound up or all strung out. Its world is full of ups and downs. Much of its time is spent going around in circles. Sometimes, it's tied up in knots. Worst of all, it's expected to perform tricks while it "sleeps." Despite all those obstacles, a yo-yo is happiest when it's wrapped around someone's finger (especially yours!). Year in and year out, yo-yos provide fun and excitement for millions of people all around the world.

Like a beloved pet, a yo-yo can be your lifelong companion. It's always ready to play when you are. It doesn't eat much (just an occasional string). It won't "bite" you (unless you want it to), and it will always come back (unless the string breaks). A yo-yo doesn't care if you're a boy or a girl, right-handed, left-handed, tall, short, fat, skinny, rich, or poor. You don't have to be athletic. You can play with a yo-yo alone or with your friends. Best of all, a yo-yo can go anywhere you go. It can easily hide inside your pocket or pack, ready to come out and be put through its paces at a moment's notice.

Here's something you should know: anyone can learn how to perform tricks with a yo-yo. All it takes is some practice, patience, and a little imagination. Start with the basic tricks, like the Gravity Pull and the Sleeper. Once you've mastered those, you'll find the key to performing many of the more complicated tricks, like Walk the Dog and Shoot the Moon. With a little more practice, you'll amaze your friends with string tricks, like Rock the Baby and Shooting Star.

On the finger of a determined player, the yo-yo can be a handful of magic. With a flick of the wrist, a yo-yo flies through the air, defying gravity as it loops and soars at the end of its string. Then, with a deft pull, it snaps back into the player's hand. The great champions make it look easy, but their skills took hours and hours of practice.

Many of today's most skilled players were bitten by the yo-yo bug as they watched champions perform. Once they picked up a yo-yo, they found they couldn't put it down. When that happens to you, you'll find yourself entering a place that avid "yoers" describe as the "state of yo." And always remember the golden rule— "Yo for it!"

A yo-yo can go anywhere you go!

CHAPTER 1

History of the YO-YO

Historians and yo-yo masters have spent countless hours trying to discover where and when the yo-yo was invented. The general conclusion is that no one knows for sure. Finding ancient information on the yo-yo is a difficult task because some yo-yo history has been lost over time. The yo-yo has also been the object of some wild myths over the years, making its origins very murky indeed.

It's generally accepted that the yo-yo began its long career in China. Approximately 2,500 years ago (give or take a few hundred years), Chinese children played with a grooved axle stuck between two crude disks made of wood, bone, or stone. For "string," they may have used a plant vine that was tied tightly to the axle. This allowed the yo-yo to do a few things—like go down and come back up—very well, and it could perform some looping tricks. So, as far as we know, the ancient yo-yo was okay for passing the time but not so great for spinning tricks like Walk the Dog or Around the World. Those tricks would have to wait thousands of years to be invented.

One thing we know for sure: the ancient Chinese didn't call their whirling gizmo a yo-yo. As a matter of fact, we don't know what they called it because no one thought to write it down! The name *yo-yo* would have to wait until the Filipinos got their hands on it hundreds of years later.

The Greeks Get Yoing

From China, the yo-yo migrated to Greece. We know this because there are drawings preserved on the sides of vases from 500 B.C.of Greek men playing with yo-yos. We owe the Greeks thanks for giving their up-and-down toy a name. They called it a *disk.*

No one really thought to keep careful yo-yo records back then. Maybe the emperors from Rome, the armies of the Crusades, the scourge of the Black Plague, and other roving hoards of blood-thirsty conquerors kept ancient historians from recording the antics of their true love—the wondrous disk. But the yo-yo spun on, even though very little was written about it. Then, in the late eighteenth century, the yo-yo popped up smack in the midst of European high society.

France Catches the Bug

The French people of the 1700s called their up-and-down toy the *incroyable,* the *quiz,* or the *jou-jou*. At the time, it was a fashionable plaything for aristocratic adults as well as children. It is said that Marie Antoinette's son was an accomplished quiz kid. Unfortunately, the French yo-yo frenzy ended during the years of terror in the French Revolution. When the government was toppled and King Louis XVI was beheaded, the yo-yo fad came to a sudden halt. Scared for their lives, the aristocrats fled the country in such a hurry, they left their *incroyables* behind. For that reason, the *incroyable*

Louis XVII, one of the original "quiz" kids.

(literally meaning "incredible") also became known as the *émigrant* (same as the English "emigrant," one who leaves one's country). Later on, the *émigrant* became the diversion of choice for Napoleon's army.

The Prince of Wales Takes to the YO-YO

In the early 1800s, the toy became known as the *bandalore*. It was the toy of choice for English royalty. There is even a painting in a British museum of the future King George IV playing with his beloved bandalore. In fact, he was so famous for his yo-yo talent, the English dubbed the bandalore the "Prince of Wales Toy." Old George probably didn't play so much after he became king, thus sparing the Prince of Wales Toy from being dubbed the "King George IV Toy."

Filipino Fingers Tame the YO-YO

The yo-yo invaded the Philippines in the early 1500s. The story goes that the Filipinos developed the yo-yo as a hunting weapon. In theory, a hunter would perch in the branches of a tree, wait for a choice animal to pass, and then spin down a rock tethered to a strong length of vine or animal tendon at the intended prey. If the hunter missed, the yo-yo would return, and the hunter could hunt again.

Unfortunately, the story doesn't hold up in the face of the facts. Ask yourself this: would you want a heavy rock slinging back into your hand? It's likely that the yo-yo as we know it today was never used to

An early advertisement for the Goody "Filipino Twirler."

hunt. It is known, however, that the Filipinos gave this little round disk and string device the name that would forever describe it—yo-yo. It's a Tagalog (Filipino) word that means literally "come, come" (although it is also interpreted as "come back"). We owe the Filipinos a great deal of gratitude for their work with the yo-yo, because without them, the yo-yo as we now know it probably wouldn't exist.

Pedro Flores and His Magical YO-YO

The biggest step in yo-yo evolution was taken in the early 1920s. A Filipino immigrant to the United States named Pedro Flores perfected a way of attaching the string to the yo-yo by looping it around the axle. The loop allowed the yo-yo to "sleep," or spin freely at the end of the string. With a subtle tug from the finger, the yo-yo would return to the hand. Once the yo-yo was sleeping, tricks could be performed with it. Demand for Pedro Flores's yo-yos got so high, he started his own company. But he didn't advertise on radio or in newspapers. To get people to buy yo-yos, he traveled around the state of California, demonstrating yo-yo tricks to anyone who would watch. Audiences were intrigued, and word-of-mouth publicity brought out ever-larger crowds. Soon a new craze was born—the yo-yo craze!

Donald F. Duncan Makes a Go at the YO-YO

Pedro Flores was doing pretty well with his wooden yo-yo, but one person who watched Pedro put his yo-yo through its paces was particularly intrigued. Donald F. Duncan saw great

Donald F. Duncan was the mastermind behind popularizing the yo-yo.

potential in the Flores-designed yo-yo. In fact, he was so enamored, he bought Flores's invention. In 1928, Duncan, the inventor of Good Humor ice cream on a stick (hooray!) and the parking meter (boooo!), made Pedro Flores an offer he couldn't refuse. Duncan knew he could market the yo-yo and make it into a business. And he did, too! Soon the Duncan name became synonymous with the yo-yo.

Ups and Downs of the YO-YO Wars

During the 1930s, 1940s, 1950s, and part of the 1960s, Donald Duncan's company held the lion's share of the yo-yo market. One reason it did was that no other company could use the name "yo-yo." Competitors had to settle for advertising their products as "bandalores," "Filipino twirlers," or "return tops," even though they were exactly like Duncan yo-yos. Over the years, competitors sued for the right to call their toys yo-yos. Finally, in 1965, after a long court battle between Duncan and his competitors, a judge ruled that the term *yo-yo* was so much a part of the public domain that Duncan had to let other companies use it.

CHAPTER 2

YO-YO Basics

If everybody loved one kind of yo-yo, there would be only one yo-yo company. But if you look around, you'll see many kinds of yo-yos in stores today. Duncan—now owned by Flambeau Products—still makes plastic yo-yos, like the Imperial, the Butterfly, the Professional, the Wheel, and the Neo. Another company, Playmaxx, markets the Pro-Yo II. Tom Kuhn Yo-Yos of San Francisco sells a line of high-quality wooden yo-yos, such as the No-Jive 3-in-1 or the SB (Silver Bullet) 2 metal yo-yo, and the Roller Woody Ball-Bearing. Another company, called Yomega, offers the Brain, the Power Spin, and the Fireball, among others. Oliver Toys sells the high-quality yo-yos Terminator and Terminator Tornado

Ball-Bearing Yo-Yo. BC (Brad Countryman) crafts moderately priced, high-quality yo-yos. And Jack Russell is the supplier to Coca-Cola for all their yo-yo promotions. His yo-yos are plastic, with wooden axles, and are considered excellent loopers.

YO-YO Types

Yo-yos are usually made of wood or plastic. Some have metal axles, while others have wood axles. Today, there are four basic yo-yo designs on the market.

1. Traditional yo-yo: Also known as the Imperial. The yo-yo that comes with this book is an example of the Imperial design. Imperials are based on the tried-and-true Duncan design of the 1930s. They usually consist of two or four pieces (counting the string as a piece).

2. Butterfly: If you take apart a traditional yo-yo and put the halves

back on backwards, you've got
a Butterfly. It's a simple differ-
ence, but when the Butterfly yo-
yos first came out, they sold like
crazy! The Butterfly is forgiving
in string tricks.

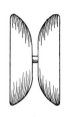

3. Rim-weighted: This yo-yo is
weighted heavily toward the outside of
the yo-yo halves, which gives the yo-yo
a longer spinning (sleeping) time.
Some come with metal rims that can
be added for even more outside
weight. An example of a rim-weighted
yo-yo is Yomega's Pro-Yo, which holds
the record for the longest sleep by a
nontransaxle yo-yo.

4. Transaxle: The transaxle yo-yo is
the latest trend in yo-yo development.
Yo-yo lover Tom Kuhn perfected this
handy little spinning machine approximately ten years ago. The other three
types of yo-yo work with a loop of string
around the axle. On a transaxle yo-yo,

the string is attached to a sleeve that surrounds the axle and rotates on ball bearings. This cuts down 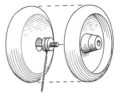 on friction and gives the transaxle yo-yo amazing spinning power, a great help in string tricks but not for looping tricks.

Another transaxle design features a mechanism inside known as a "clutch." When this type of yo-yo (see below) is spinning quickly, the clutch releases, allowing the yo-yo to spin freely. As the yo-yo slows down, the clutch eventually grabs the string and the yo-yo automatically returns to the hand.

Many players believe that the transaxle yo-yo is a great tool for beginners because it can spin for such a long time. If you want to learn string tricks with less effort than a traditional-style yo-yo requires, the transaxle is for you.

How Are YO-YOS Made?

In the 1920s, yo-yos were usually hand carved from a single piece of wood. The people who made them often cut designs as well as their names in the sides. The yo-yos were excellent, but they couldn't be made in large numbers. Every yo-yo made by hand was like no other.

Donald Duncan changed all that. In a short time, he was turning out thousands of yo-yos to a very eager public. To increase production, Duncan bought wood lathes to cut out his yo-yos. Every yo-yo was shaped to precise specifications. And Duncan used a special wood called rock maple. (If you ever get bonked by a yo-yo in a tender spot, you'll know why it is called "rock" maple.) He needed so much of this wood, he moved his manufacturing plant to a town in Wisconsin, called Luck, that was full of rock maple trees. So many yo-yos were produced in Luck that it became known as the Yo-Yo Capital of the World. Duncan's own luck held out for over 30 years.

In the late 1960s, Flambeau Products bought Duncan's company. Flambeau specialized in making items from plastic, so plastic became its yo-yo material of choice. The use of plastic sped up production of yo-yos, and plastic also allowed Flambeau to make see-through yo-yos, colored yo-yos, and yo-yos with sparkles in them.

Plastic yo-yos are created in a process called injection molding. Plastic, much of it recycled, is melted down. Then the hot plastic goop is injected into molds shaped like yo-yo halves. As soon as the hot plastic has cooled, the halves are released. Workers smooth off the edges, join the halves with an axle (most often made of metal), attach a string, and then the process begins all over again. Lots of yo-yos can be made very quickly this way.

The yo-yo that comes with this book is a traditional yo-yo made of wood. Most yo-yos today are generally made of wood or plastic. A traditional yo-yo usually consists of either two or four pieces (counting the string as one of the pieces).

Like the early yo-yos, some are cut from a single piece of wood, while others have a metal or wood axle firmly glued between the two plastic or wooden halves. These yo-yos are called *fixed axle* yo-yos because they don't come apart. The yo-yo that comes with this book has a fixed axle, so never take it apart.

Most yo-yos before the 1980s were made in the fixed-axle design. When the axle broke, however, the yo-yo was finished. Then Tom Kuhn, owner of Tom Kuhn Yo-Yos Ltd., pioneered the take-apart, or dismountable, yo-yo.

These yo-yos are designed to open up for easy maintenance. Simply unscrew the halves, and you can replace a broken axle or a worn string without breaking a sweat. In the evolution of the yo-yo, this was a major step.

How Does a YO-YO Work?

A yo-yo works on a couple of pretty simple principles: momentum and friction. Unleashing a good throw gives the yo-yo momentum by transferring energy from the arm and wrist into the yo-yo, making it rotate at high speed in the direction of the throw. When a yo-yo reaches the end of its string, it still contains the energy from the momentum of the throw, so it spins inside the loop either until it runs out of spin or until you tug it to make it climb back up the string into your hand.

The loop around the yo-yo's axle allows the yo-yo to sleep without return-

ing to your hand. When you tug the yo-yo, the string momentarily grabs the axle. The grab is the result of a brief increase in friction, which initiates the yo-yo's return trip. Once the axle grabs the string, the yo-yo obeys the laws of physics and climbs back into your hand.

YO-YO Safety

Now that you're on the verge of "yo-hood," keep a few things in mind:

• Practice tricks where the yo-yo will be flying around, like the Forward Pass, outside, away from non-yo-yo-proof items like vases, windows, or fine china. Flying yo-yos have been known to conk the player's head, bruise hands, blister fingers, and knock out teeth, as well as break things.

• Be thoughtful of others. Don't yo-yo too close to other people or fling the yo-yo in the direction of others. A moving yo-yo or a swinging "dead" yo-yo can make people uncomfortable, and it can be dangerous.

If you yo-yo a lot, your fingers may develop blisters. While this may be painful, it will help in the long run. You'll develop highly prized and highly respected yo-yo calluses.

What Will YO-YOing Do for Me?

With practice, you'll learn how to control your yo-yo. You may not be able to master Splitting the Atom for a long time, but you'll find immense satisfaction in Walking the Dog and Looping the Loop. Learning how to yo is a matter of breaking tricks down into stages. The basic methods for completing a yo-yo trick are easily learned. Getting your yo-yo to sleep for extended periods of time opens the door to many other tricks (like Around the World and the Shooting Star). You can also learn how to

arrange the string in seemingly complicated webs and ultimately learn how to use two yo-yos at the same time. If you take the time to learn the basics properly, you will go on to perform most tricks without too much frustration. But take it slow at first. Get used to the simple tricks before going on to the more difficult ones.

All your yo-yo asks of you is that you spend time learning how to use it (and give it a new string from time to time). In return, your yo-yo will teach you how to sharpen your hand-eye coordination. You'll learn patience, and best of all, you'll feel the exhilaration of learning a skill that will never leave you.

The yo-yo can be a great social tool. Try yo-ing in a public place and see how many people come up and tell you how they used to be able to Skin the Cat and Loop the Loop. It's hard not to watch when someone is putting the yo-yo through its paces. So beware when you take out your yo-yo: you just might make some new friends.

Holding Your YO-YO

1. Put the finger loop around your middle finger, halfway between your first and second knuckle.

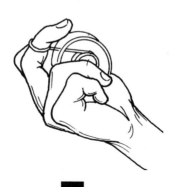

2. Turn your palm up. The string should go from under your finger to the side of the yo-yo axle closest to your body. Yoers in the know call this "over the top."

3. Bend your arm up toward your ear. (Remember, your hand is palm up.) Your hand should then be cocked right by your jaw.

4. Holding the yo-yo tightly in your hand, bring your arm down. Snap your wrist back and down, and let the yo-yo roll over the length of your fingers and loop outward. This gives the string a bit of a loop as the yo-yo falls. The yo-yo will hurl itself down toward the end of its string.

5. Just before the yo-yo reaches the end of its string, turn your hand over. If you have thrown the yo-yo straight down, it will come right back up.

Try not to throw your yo-yo too hard. A nice, easy motion is all it takes to perform many of the tricks. And don't be discouraged if your yo-yo doesn't sleep or you fail to catch the yo-yo as it comes back. You will get it with practice.

Ready, Set, YO

Now that you've mastered the basics, you're probably eager to start learning tricks. With your yo-yo, you will begin to learn tricks that have been practiced and perfected for generations. And slowly but surely, your yo-yo will turn into a trusty and handy companion. Someday, you may be cleaning out your desk and you'll find your trusty old yo-yo. You'll wind up the string, throw the yo-yo down, and find to your delight that you can still make it do some tricks.

Learning yo-yo tricks can be frustrating, especially as you get more advanced. In addition to studying the illustrations in this book, it's very helpful to join a yo-yo club or attend a yo-yo competition. Many tricks are handed down from skilled yoers to beginners. The key is to *want* to learn. A hungry interest in yo-ing will allow you to have fun while you develop your skills.

Many of the more complicated tricks require a great deal of practice and repetition until the movements of the yo-yo are natural. In time, you won't even have to think about an Outside Loop or Shoot the Moon. Your yo-yo will respond to your movements like an extension of your arm. As long as your yo-yo is in good condition and your string is in good shape, you'll be limited only by what you can accomplish. Remember, "Old yo-yos never die. They just play out the string."

CHAPTER 3

YO-YO Lingo

As you find yourself spinning deeper and deeper into the yo-yo world, you'll want to converse with other yoers. Yo-yo lingo is pretty simple, and there isn't much of it. However, a few words will help you learn the tricks and teach them to others.

Fixed-axle yo-yo: A yo-yo designed not to be taken apart. The yo-yo that comes with this book is a fixed-axle yo-yo.

Dismountable yo-yo: Also known as a **take apart.** This is a type of yo-yo with an axle that screws into one of the halves. It makes changing the string a little easier.

All you need is a flat surface to "Walk the Dog."

Transaxle: This is the new yo-yo on the block. It doesn't spin inside a string loop; rather, the string is attached to a sleeve mounted on tiny ball bearings. This sleeve surrounds the center axle, thereby reducing friction. This permits the transaxle yo-yo to spin for a long time.

Fly-away: What happens when your string breaks and the yo-yo zooms off to points unknown.

Sleeper: Also called a **Spinner**. When the yo-yo spins freely in its loop at the end of its string.

Dead yo-yo: This is a yo-yo that's not spinning but is just hanging there.

Combination: Two or more yo-yo tricks performed back-to-back, such as a Forward Pass (see page 70) followed by an Inside Loop (see page 76).

String tricks: These tricks require the yoer to use the string as part of the trick. Rock the Baby (see page 84) is a string trick because you maneuver the string into a triangle. For a string trick to work, the yo-yo must remain spinning throughout the whole exercise. Then, when you let go of the string, the yo-yo should have enough spin to return to your hand.

Looping tricks: Looping tricks require the yoer to put the yo-yo through a series of maneuvers that send it away and back to the yo-yoer's hand. Examples of looping tricks are the Orbit Launch (see page 87), the Three-Leaf Clover (see page 95), and Outside Loop (see page 74).

Brain: This is the term for a transaxle yo-yo with a "clutch" mechanism. When a yo-yo spins fast enough, the force of the spin releases the "clutch" and allows the yo-yo to stay at the end of its string. When the yo-yo's spin slows down, the "clutch" grabs the string and the yo-yo returns automatically to your hand.

Yoer: As soon as you learn a few yo-yo tricks, you are known as a "yoer."

The infamous dog "bite."

41

CHAPTER 4

Strings and Things

I t can be argued that the yo-yo string is more important than the yo-yo itself. After all, you and the string do all the work. The yo-yo just hangs out and throws its weight around. So being familiar with all aspects of the string will save you hours of frustration.

Once you catch the yo-yo bug, you'll go through countless strings, unravel all kinds of crazy knots, rewind your yo-yo thousands of times, and tie hundreds of finger knots. So really learn the basics first. Then you won't have to worry when your yo-yo flies off a worn string (unless it goes through a window). All you have to do is replace the string and get back to the important business of yo-ing.

When Should I Replace My String?

Yo-yo string doesn't last forever. As you get better at yo-ing, you'll realize that you have to replace the string more and more often. Because the string is looped around the yo-yo's axle, friction is created when the yo-yo is spinning. Friction creates heat. As the yo-yo spins faster and faster, more heat is given off. In time, the heat does one of two things. It either burns through the string or burns through the wooden axle! When either one of these things happens, look out! So if your yo-yo string is getting frayed, change it.

A knot in your string will prevent you from performing even the most simple yo-yo tricks. Sometimes you can work a knot out; other times you can't.

It's all part of a string's life cycle. One moment, your string is fine; the next, your string is knotted. Knots make you miserable and wreck even the most basic tricks. Once you get a knot in the string that you can't work out, the string's had it. Replace it!

If your string breaks, don't tie it back together. Replace it with a new string. Lots of beginners break strings and tie the pieces together. Then they get frustrated, complain that their yo-yos are broken, and give up.

Most popular yo-yo strings are made from long fibers of Egyptian cotton, and cotton strings get dirty. Other strings that don't get dirty have come and gone, but nothing has ever replaced good old cotton string. When your string gets dirty, replace it. Yo-yos love new string!

Buy new real yo-yo strings in advance so you'll have them on hand when you need them. Nothing's more frustrating than waiting weeks for new string to arrive and making do with a poor substitute in the meantime. You're going to have to replace your string eventually, so you might as well get it over with. You'll be glad you did!

Where to Get New Strings

Precut and prelooped strings are easy to use and convenient to buy. Here's where you can get precut strings.

Yomega yo-yo strings:
String made from cotton fibers. Five strings in a pack ($1.75). Available from Yomega.

Duncan strings:
String made from cotton fibers. Five strings in a pack (#3276NP, $1.75). Available from Duncan (Flambeau Products).

BC multicolored yo-yo strings:
Cotton yo-yo string in cool colors. Five strings in a pack ($2.00). Available from BC.

Playmaxx strings:
String made from cotton fibers. Bag of three (75 cents) or 100 count bulk ($12.00). Available from Playmaxx.

String on a Spool

Yo-yo string can be bought wrapped around a large spool. Many yo-yo professionals buy string on a spool because it allows them to cut the string to the length they prefer.

If you'd like to try this way of stringing your yo-yo, here's how to do it:

1. Put your yo-yo down between your feet. In one hand, hold the string spool 2–3 inches above your waist.

2. Unspool enough string to reach from the spool to the axle of your yo-yo and back up to the spool.

3. Take the end of the string and thread it around the axle of your grounded yo-yo, then bring the end back up to a point 2–3 inches above your waist.

4. Hold the big long loop tight and cut the string away from the spool.

5. Hold both ends of the string together with one hand, then spin your yo-yo with the other. The pair of strands will twist together into one string.

6. Tie a finger loop (see page 53).

Tom Kuhn Yo-Yos Ltd. sells string spools. Each spool provides enough length for five or six strings. Write or call Tom Kuhn Yo-Yos for information (see page 145).

How Long Should My String Be?

If your yo-yo string is too long, your yo-yo will bounce off the floor and ruin your tricks. If it's too short, your yo-yo won't be able to perform certain tricks. So how long should your string be? The rule of thumb is that the string should reach from your belly button down to the yo-yo as it touches the floor.

How Do I Replace the String?

Strings have a habit of wearing out in two places: around your finger and around the yo-yo axle. Replacing the string is probably the trickiest phase of yo-yo maintenance, so *take your time* when you're learning.

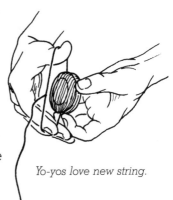

Yo-yos love new string.

After you replace your string a few times, it will become as easy as tying your shoelaces. If you don't understand the instructions, ask an adult to help you. (But watch out when you ask an adult to hold your yo-yo. The person might want to try a few tricks before returning it to you!)

The yo-yo that comes with this book is not meant to be taken apart. If you pull the yo-yo halves apart and then just press them together again, your yo-yo will probably fly apart during some trick. So don't open up your yo-yo. To replace your string, work the twist out of the bottom of the string until it splits. An easy way to do this is to hold the string 3 or 4 inches above the yo-yo with a thumb and forefinger, and with your other hand, twist the yo-yo around and around until the string unravels. When the string is suitably untwisted, gently work the yo-yo out from between the strands of untwisted string.

To put on a new piece of string, untwist the strands at the loop that will go around the axle. Open up the two strands with your finger until the opening is just big enough to slide your yo-yo through it. Now twist the strands back together into one string, and your yo-yo is ready for action.

Adjusting Your YO-YO String

If the string loop around the axle of your yo-yo is too tight (below), the yo-yo won't sleep; if it's too loose (right), the yo-yo won't return to your hand. As soon as your new string is on your yo-yo, check the loop to see if there's a little play (extra room) between the string and the axle.

Throw the yo-yo down. If it comes right back without sleeping, then the string is too tight. Loosen the string by holding it with one hand and then twisting the yo-yo around a few times *counterclockwise* with the other hand. Throw the yo-yo down again. If it's still too tight, repeat the counterclockwise twist.

If the yo-yo refuses to come back, the string is too loose. Let the yo-yo hang, and this time twist the yo-yo *clockwise*. This will tighten the string.

Make sure you use genuine yo-yo string. Years of experimentation have proved over and over that only a yo-yo string works right on a yo-yo.

How Do I Tie My Finger Loop?

There are several ways to tie a slipknot for your finger, but here is a simple method.

1. Make a small loop.

2. Take the end of the string, curl it around, and then knot it to the loop.

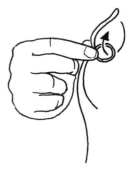

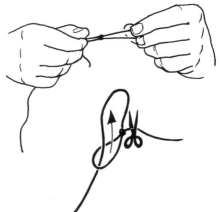

3. Put the loop around the middle finger of your yo-yo hand and pull it snug.

Winding the String

Here is a good way to wind the string in your yo-yo.

1. Holding your yo-yo in one hand, with your forefinger covering the center groove, wind the string *away* from you.

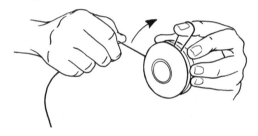

2. Place your forefinger over the yo-yo's opening, then wind the string over your finger a couple of times.

3. Gently remove your finger from the opening and wind the rest of the string around tight. Your yo-yo is now armed and ready!

Tight-String Tricks
vs. Loose-String Tricks

Sometimes, a tight or loose string isn't such a bad thing. For spinning tricks like Around the World and Rock the Baby, it helps to loosen the string a bit, giving the yo-yo a little more room to spin.

Tight-string tricks include handling tricks like Hop the Fence, Outside Loops, and Forward Pass.

If you're right-handed, you will find that performing tricks like Outside Loops tends to tighten your string. This means, as you go along, that the string will tighten around the axle, thus reducing your yo-yo's sleeping abilities. If you are left-handed and perform the same tricks, the opposite will occur: the string will loosen.

Some tricks tighten string and others loosen string. As you get more skilled with your yo-yo, you'll learn to alternate string-loosening tricks with string-tightening tricks.

CHAPTER 5

Trick Time

You've got your yo-yo. You've wound your string around the axle. You're ready to go. Now comes the challenging and fun part—learning tricks.

Don't be discouraged if you can't get your yo-yo to perform the way you want it to right away. It helps to picture the tricks in your mind. Sometimes, your body reacts better when you can "see" and "feel" how a trick should be carried out. In due time, you'll be doing the Gravity Pull, Walk the Dog, and Forward Pass.

Some tricks are very easy, and some may seem impossible, but they're all possible if you take the time and patience to learn them. Here, they're all coded so you can tell how difficult they are at a glance:

Basic Must be learned in order to do more difficult tricks

Level 1 Takes a lot of practice

Level 2 Hard

Level 3 Really hard

Level 4 Master level

Keep in mind that there are as many yo-yo tricks as the imagination can produce. This book does not contain every trick, but part of the fun of yo-ing is inventing new ones or trying out different combinations of tricks. Just like any instrument in the hands of an artist, your only obstacles are the physical limitations of your yo-yo and your mind.

BASIC TRICKS

GRAVITY PULL
(AKA POWER THROW)
Basic

This simple trick is the basis for many other tricks. Keep practicing the Gravity Pull until you can do several in a row.

1. Stand with your yo-yo in your hand, palm up, gripping the yo-yo fairly tightly. The loop of the string should be snug between the first and second knuckle of your middle finger. The string should go from the bottom of your finger over the axle of the yo-yo.

2. Place your throwing hand at ear level and bring your arm straight down in a quick motion.

3. Release the yo-yo by letting go with your thumb and allowing the yo-yo to roll aross the length of your fingers.

4. As the yo-yo reaches the end of its string, quickly turn your hand over, palm down. Give the string a light tug, and the yo-yo will return to your hand.

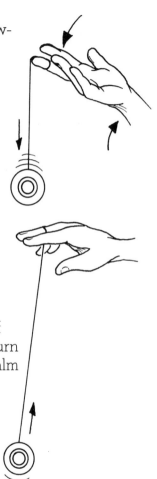

SLEEPER (AKA SPINNER)
Basic

When you're comfortable with getting your yo-yo to go down and return, learn the Sleeper. This trick is a must for any and all string tricks. At first, your yo-yo will sleep for only a second or two before you tug it back to your hand. And you may have trouble catching the returning yo-yo at first. In time, this will feel natural. The trick is to develop your arm-wrist snap so that you can get the yo-yo to sleep for 4 to 5 seconds. You'll then be able to increase the sleeping time. The longer your yo-yo spins, the more tricks you will be able to do. For many yo-yo tricks, a spinning time of 8 to 10 seconds is sufficient.

1. As you throw your yo-yo down, relax your hand and wrist. This will allow the string to give a little bit. By doing this,

you buffer the yo-yo's
downward force.
The yo-yo will spin,
or sleep, at the
end of the string.

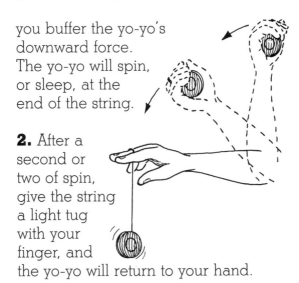

2. After a
second or
two of spin,
give the string
a light tug
with your
finger, and
the yo-yo will return to your hand.

If the yo-yo doesn't make it all the
way up the string, reduce its sleeping
time. If it refuses to sleep and keeps
coming right back, check the tension
of your string (see page 52). With
practice, you'll be able to get your yo-
yo to sleep for longer and longer periods of time. When getting the yo-yo to
sleep feels comfortable to you, move
on to the next trick.

WALK THE DOG
Basic

This is a fun trick because your yo-yo acts like a dog going for a walk, hence the name. A wood or tile surface is best. This trick doesn't work on a rug!

1. Throw a nice, strong sleeper and let your yo-yo down nice and slow until it barely touches the floor. Like a frisky dog, the yo-yo will roll forward.

2. After a few seconds of "walking," tug the yo-yo back into your hand.

BUZZ SAW
Basic

This trick is a variation of Walk the Dog. Instead of letting the yo-yo down on a smooth surface, use a newspaper.

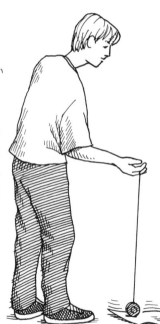

1. Begin with a fast sleeper, lowering the yo-yo onto a newspaper. When the yo-yo hits the newspaper, it will make a buzzing sound.

2. After a few seconds of buzz, tug the string and return the yo-yo to your hand.

CREEPER

(AKA LAND ROVER)

Basic

This trick uses the same technique as Walk the Dog.

1. Throw a strong sleeper and let your yo-yo "walk" on the floor in front of you, just as in Walk the Dog.

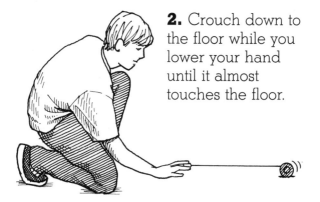

2. Crouch down to the floor while you lower your hand until it almost touches the floor.

3. Give the yo-yo a tug to return it to your hand.

LEVEL 1 TRICKS

JUMP THE DOG THROUGH THE HOOP
Level 1

This trick is a variation of Walk the Dog. You Walk the Dog not in front of you, but *behind* you.

1. Throw a nice, strong sleeper. Put your yo-yo hand behind your back, and let the "dog" walk forward between your legs.

2. Place your yo-yo hand on your hip and give the string a little tug. The yo-yo will run around the string, up your leg, through the "hoop" you've made with your arm, and back into your hand.

FORWARD PASS
Level 1

Try not to overthrow your yo-yo on this trick. The harder you throw it, the faster it will come back. A nice, gentle throwing motion is all you need.

1. Hold the yo-yo in your hand as for the Gravity Pull. Make sure the string on your yo-yo is over the top.

2. Keeping your arm straight, swing it behind your back. The motion to perform this trick is the same as for throwing a softball underhanded, except that your palm faces to the rear.

3. Swing your arm forward and release the yo-yo behind your back

just before your arm reaches your side,
letting the yo-yo roll off your fingers.
The yo-yo will drop, then rise in a loop
and return to your hand.

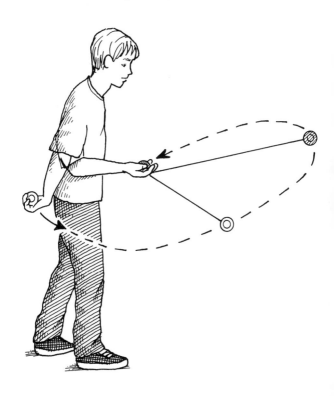

LATERAL PASS
Level 1

In the Lateral Pass, your throw goes out to the left or right, instead of down, and then returns to your hand.

1. Hold the yo-yo in your hand with your palm open to the left if you're right-handed, to the right if you're left-handed.

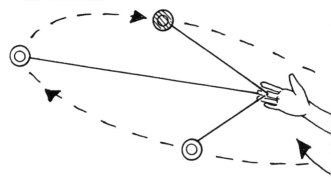

2. Give the yo-yo a good sleeper throw sideways to your right if you're right-handed, to your left if you're left-handed. The yo-yo should go out sideways and then come spinning back into your hand.

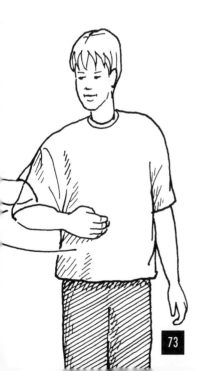

OUTSIDE LOOP
(AKA ASTRO LOOP AND LOOP THE LOOP)
Level 1

The yo-yo moves very quickly in this trick. Done correctly, an Outside Loop comes and goes in the blink of an eye! Keep your hand away from your body or the yo-yo might come straight back toward your face.

1. Throw the yo-yo as you would for a Forward Pass, but as the yo-yo comes toward you, don't catch it. Instead, turn your hand to face out. The yo-yo will pass on the outside of your arm.

2. To send it out again, swing the yo-yo forward by moving your wrist in a tight circle.

3. To catch the yo-yo, tug your finger.

Good yo-yo players can keep an Outside Loop going and going. Another trick, Loop the Loop, is just an Outside Loop that you repeat over and over. As long as you feel you can do another cycle when the yo-yo returns from the loop, keep going!

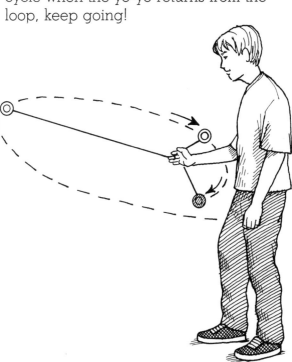

INSIDE LOOP
(AKA LUNAR LOOP)
Level 1

If you've mastered the Outside Loop, the Inside Loop should be a snap!

1. Throw a Forward Pass and stretch out your arm. When the yo-yo comes back, don't catch it. Instead, let it go around the *inside* of your wrist.

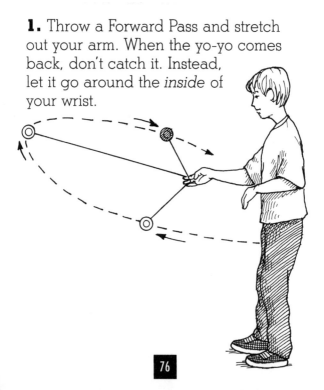

2. Now twist your wrist forward in a circular motion. The yo-yo will loop around your hand and then keep going.

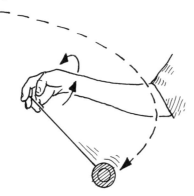

3. To catch the yo-yo, tug the string.

OVER THE FALLS
Level 1

1. Begin this trick with a Forward Pass throw.

2. When the yo-yo comes back, don't catch it. Curve your wrist. This will direct the yo-yo to go down.

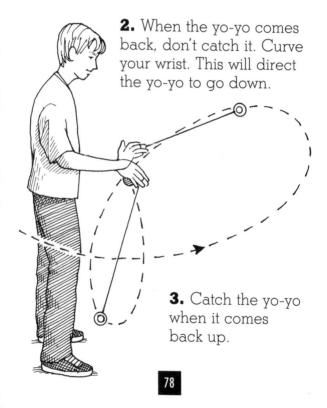

3. Catch the yo-yo when it comes back up.

78

DRAGSTER
Level 1

This is a fun trick to learn if you have pets. If you do it correctly, your dog or cat will chase your yo-yo all over the house!

1. Throw down a good, hard sleeper.

2. Gently work the loop off your finger and lower your yo-yo to the floor.

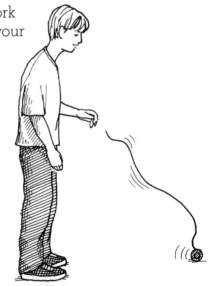

3. Let go of the yo-yo. It will take off along the floor like a rocket—with your pet in hot pursuit!

BREAKAWAY
Level 1

1. Throw a good sleeper, dropping it to the outside of your yo-yo hand.

2. Swing the yo-yo out so that it crosses in front of you, going from your yo-yo-hand shoulder to your opposite shoulder.

3. As soon as the yo-yo reaches the opposite shoulder, give the string a little pull, and the yo-yo will come back.

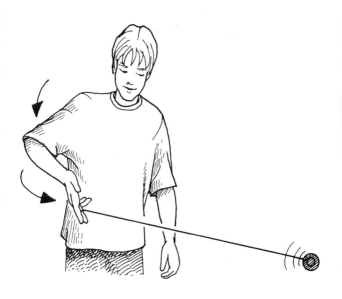

AROUND THE WORLD
Level 1

You need lots of space to perform this trick, so you should probably do it outside—away from any bystanders.

1. Begin this trick the same way you would a Breakaway, but bend your elbow slightly.

2. When the yo-yo reaches your non-yo-yo shoulder, don't bring it back. Let it go until it makes a complete circle.

3. As soon as you've completed a loop, tug the yo-yo to return it to your hand.

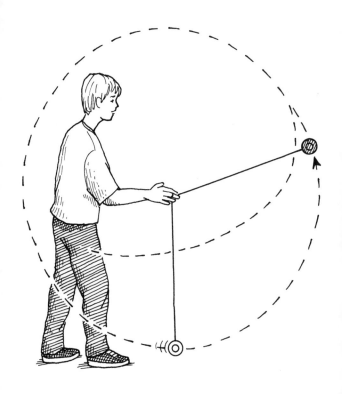

ROCK THE BABY
Level 1

Everybody loves showing off this trick! To get used to making the "cradle," try it first with a dead yo-yo. This trick needs a 6- to 8-second sleeper to work right.

1. Throw your yo-yo down in a fast sleeper, and hold your yo-yo hand out in front of you—about chest high—as if you're about to catch a ball.

2. With your free hand, grab the string that's between the thumb and forefinger of your yo-yo hand.

3. Pull down and spread your fingers at the bottom—now you have the "cradle." Gently sway your sleeper back and forth through the cradle.

4. Let go of the string, and the yo-yo will return to your hand.

DOG BITE
Level 1

This is a quick little trick that turns your yo-yo into a chomping beast. For best results, wear a pair of long, baggy pants.

1. Begin with your legs spread apart, and throw a very fast sleeper, swinging the yo-yo back and forth gently between your legs.

2. As the yo-yo swings behind you, give the string a light tug as you move your leg (on the yo-yo side).

3. If you have a good sleeper going, the yo-yo will stick to your leg and "bite" your pants.

ORBIT LAUNCH
Level 1

This impressive trick requires you to keep your sleeper going for more than 6 seconds.

1. After throwing a good, strong sleeper, bend your arm at shoulder level as if you were going to make a muscle.

2. Drape the yo-yo over your arm from back to front.

3. With your yo-yo hand back under your arm, grab the string and give it a slight upward tug. The yo-yo will follow the string over your arm, drop down in front of you, and then return to your hand.

HOP THE FENCE
(AKA PLANET HOP)
Level 1

1. This trick begins with a good, hard Gravity Pull throw.

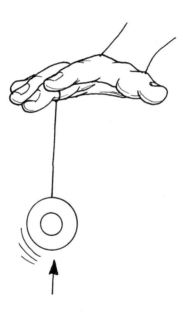

2. When the yo-yo comes back up the string, let it go over the top of your hand and it will go back down again.

3. When the yo-yo comes back up the second time, you can either catch it or send it around again.

For a Backward Hop the Fence, flick the yo-yo over the top of your hand *toward* you, then throw the yo-yo down.

ELEVATOR
Level 1

1. After throwing down a good, strong sleeper, take the forefinger of your non-yo-yo hand and put it against the string.

2. Drop the finger of your yo-yo hand down and maneuver the string into the yo-yo's opening.

3. Pull up the finger on your non-yo-yo hand while pulling down with your yo-yo-hand finger. The yo-yo will scramble up the string!

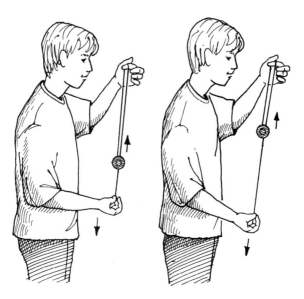

4. When the yo-yo reaches the top, pull your finger out and let the yo-yo return to your yo-yo hand.

LEVEL 2 TRICKS

I f you've gotten the hang of all the Level 1 tricks, congratulations! Here are some tricks that are a little more challenging.

BRAIN TWISTER
Level 2

1. Start by throwing down a very strong sleeper and then move the index finger of your non-yo-yo hand forward into the string.

2. Pull down with your yo-yo hand. When the yo-yo is about halfway between both hands, insert the yo-yo string inside the yo-yo.

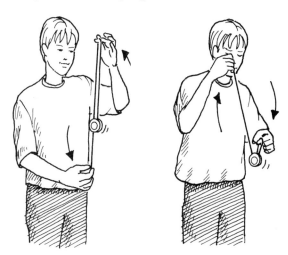

3. With the index finger of your yo-yo hand, carry the doubled string toward you and bring your non-yo-yo hand forward and down. The yo-yo will swing up and over and then down again.

(continued on next page)

4. Bring your yo-yo hand toward you while moving your other finger (and all the string) away from you. The yo-yo will spin in the opposite direction and go up, around, and off the finger of your non-yo-yo hand. As the yo-yo unwinds, it will go out in front of you and you can catch it.

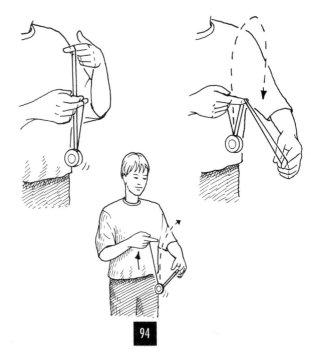

THREE-LEAF CLOVER
Level 2

This trick is a series of three Inside Loops. The first two loops are not very difficult, but getting the third loop to go straight down takes practice.

1. Throw the first loop (or leaf) up, slightly above your head.

2. Throw the second loop straight out in front of you.

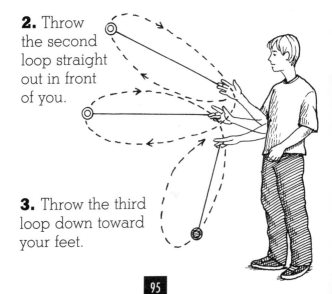

3. Throw the third loop down toward your feet.

95

GEMINI LOOPS
Level 2

Gemini Loops are two tricks done back-to-back. Multiple tricks performed together are called a combination. Gemini Loops is an Inside Loop followed by an Outside Loop. Alternate Inside Loops and Outside Loops until the yo-yo runs out of steam or your arm falls off!

The beauty of this trick is that it keeps your yo-yo string from getting too loose or too tight. Each Inside Loop tightens the string half a turn, and each Outisde Loop loosens the string half a turn.

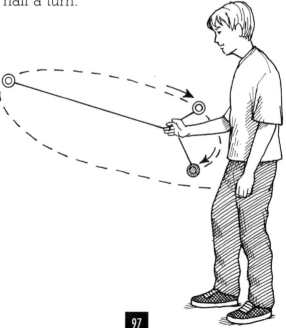

SKYROCKET
Level 2

If this trick doesn't impress your friends and loved ones, nothing will! To begin, wear a shirt with a breast pocket.

1. Throw a good, hard sleeper and gently take the string loop off your yo-yo-hand finger.

2. Pinching the string between the thumb and forefinger of your yo-yo hand, give the string a slight tug. The yo-yo will come tearing back up the string.

3. Just as the yo-yo is about to touch your fingers, let go! The yo-yo will keep going above your head, up into the air.

4. Open your shirt pocket and catch the yo-yo as it comes down.

SLEEPING BEAUTY
(AKA THE FLYING SAUCER)
Level 2

According to yo-yo champion Dale Oliver, Donald Duncan named numerous tricks after outer-space phenomena that fascinated us in the 1970s. (That's why there are so many tricks with AKAs.) This trick is appropriately nicknamed the Flying Saucer.

1. Throw the yo-yo hard to your yo-yo-hand side in a good, fast sideways sleeper.

2. As the yo-yo spins on its side, place the thumb and index finger of your non-yo-yo

hand about 8 inches above the spinning yo-yo, and slowly pull the yo-yo
up between your thumb and forefinger
to see the Flying Saucer.

3. For the big finish, flip the yo-yo up
while at the same time tugging with
your yo-yo finger.

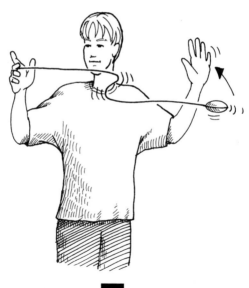

TRAPEZE

(AKA THE MAN ON THE FLYING TRAPEZE)
Level 2

I f you impressed your friends with the Skyrocket, this is an encore that will leave them speechless.

1. Throw the yo-yo as you would for an Around the World, with your palm facing down.

2. As the yo-yo begins its rise, extend your non-yo-yo-hand forefinger so that the yo-yo string swings over it onto the string.

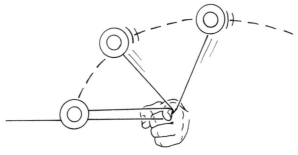

3. Gently slide the spinning yo-yo back and forth on the string.

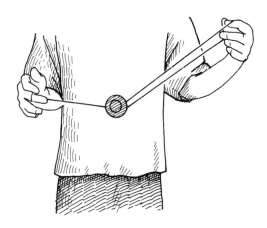

4. To finish the trick, flip the yo-yo up in the air with both hands, and it will return to your hand.

TIDAL WAVE
(AKA SKIN THE CAT)
Level 2

1. Throw down a good sleeper and stretch your hands out in front of you. (You'll need a good 6 to 8 seconds of sleeping time to make this work.)

2. With your non-yo-yo hand, reach over and touch your index finger to the string about an inch below your yo-yo hand. Pull back

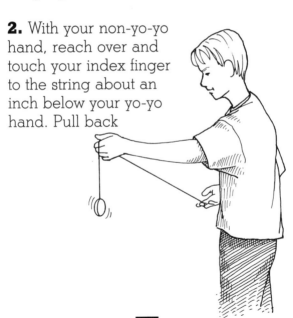

steadily with your yo-yo hand and draw the string across the finger of your non-yo-yo hand.

3. When you've pulled the sleeping yo-yo to hip level, use your free finger to flip the yo-yo up and out. The yo-yo will swing over your non-yo-yo hand and start to wind up.

(continued on next page)

4. Before the yo-yo returns to your hand, send it out into an Inner Loop and catch it when it returns to your throwing hand.

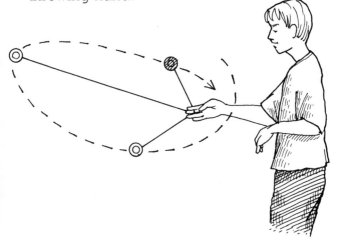

DAISY
Level 2

If you mastered the Shooting Star (see pages 110–111), the Daisy should be just a walk in the garden for you! As with the Shooting Star, you might want to practice this trick in front of a mirror.

1. After beginning with a good, strong sleeper, put the forefinger of your non-yo-yo hand out and drape the string over it.

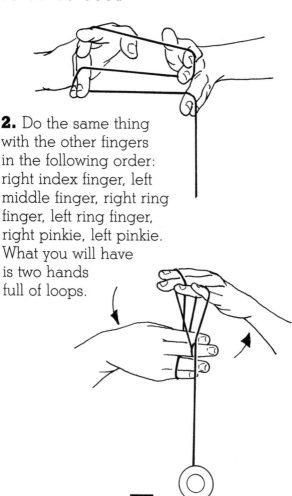

2. Do the same thing with the other fingers in the following order: right index finger, left middle finger, right ring finger, left ring finger, right pinkie, left pinkie. What you will have is two hands full of loops.

108

3. Swing the yo-yo around the middle of the loops several times, and you've turned the string into a flower.

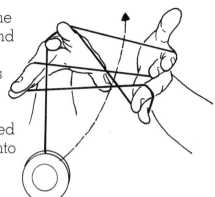

4. Release all the string at once, and the yo-yo will spin back into your hand.

SHOOTING STAR
(AKA URSA MINOR)
Level 2

This is a one-handed string trick you should try initially with a "dead" yo-yo. It's a good idea to practice in front of a mirror first. When you get the hang of getting the string around your fingers, add one heck of a strong sleeper, and you've got a great trick!

1. Begin with a strong sleeper and twist your yo-yo hand so that the string hangs on the outside of the little finger.

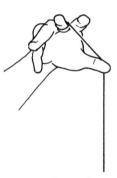

2. To make the star, turn your hand so that the string catches on the outside of your forefinger (over the nail).

3. Maneuver your hand so that the string rests on the outside of your fourth finger.

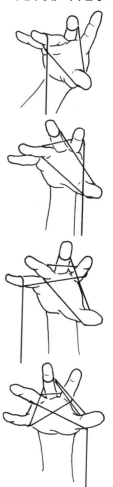

4. Turn your hand so that the string goes over the outside of your thumb, then back over your middle finger (but *under* your index finger).

5. Move your fingers so that the string forms a star.

6. To end the trick, release all the string, and the yo-yo will return to your hand.

TANDEM DOG WALK
Level 2

Welcome to the wonderful world of two-handed yo-yo tricks! You'll have to buy yourself another yo-yo for these. Once you've begun to master two-handed yo-yo tricks, you'll never turn back! Practice Walk the Dog using the hand you don't usually use for yo-ing. When you've got a pretty good Walk the Dog with each hand, you're ready.

1. With a yo-yo in each hand, throw down a pair of good, fast sleepers and place both yo-yos lightly on the floor, following the same procedure you used for Walk the Dog.

2. Give both strings a tug, and the two "dogs" will scurry back into your hands.

DOUBLE OR NOTHING
Level 2

1. Begin this trick in the same way you would begin a Trapeze (see page 102), with your arm cocked in front of you. For this to work, throw a very strong sleeper.

2. As you swing the yo-yo across your body, hold out your arms in front of you. With the index finger of your non-yo-yo hand, cut off the string about a

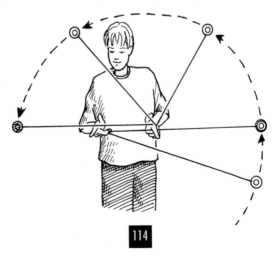

foot from your yo-yo finger. Let the
yo-yo keep going to double back and
loop around the index finger of your
throwing hand. It will continue on and
loop once again over the finger of your
non-yo-yo hand.

3. Catch the yo-yo on any one of the
three strings that you are holding
between your hands (this is the tricky
part).

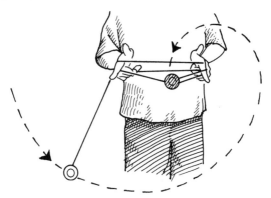

4. Complete the trick by flipping the
yo-yo off the string and letting it wind
up back into your hand.

LEVEL 3 TRICKS

PINWHEEL
Level 3

1. Throw a good, fast sleeper, and with your non-yo-yo hand, grab the string between your thumb and forefinger, leaving about 6 inches between the string and the yo-yo.

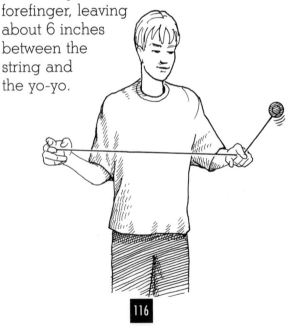

2. Swing the yo-yo around a few times in a small circle.

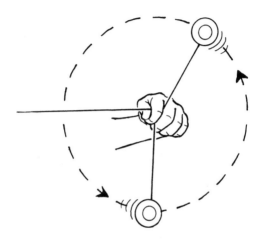

3. To return the yo-yo to your hand, let go of the string.

SPAGHETTI
Level 3

If you're this far along with your tricks and you can do them pretty easily, maybe it's time you started entertaining at birthday parties. The following trick is sure to amuse everyone.

1. Throw a good, hard sleeper, and with your non-yo-yo hand, pinch about 5 inches of string to make a small loop. Repeat this looping over and over, until you have only a few inches of string left.

2. Raise the yo-yo to your mouth. *Make sure your hand is between the yo-yo and your mouth!* Make a loud slurping noise and let the string go. It will look as if you are sucking up all the "spaghetti."

ROCK THE BABY ON THE TRAPEZE
Level 3

This is a very advanced trick, but if you've reached this point in your yo-yo evolution, nothing is impossible! You need to give yourself a long, strong sleeper to get through this trick, but practice the string maneuvering first with a dead yo-yo. If your yo-yo stops spinning before you finish, work on extending your yo-yo's sleeping time.

1. Begin with the Trapeze, swinging your yo-yo over the index finger of

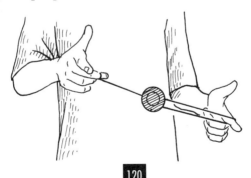

your free hand onto the string. Give yourself plenty of slack on the string leading down from your non-yo-yo hand.

2. At a point about 3 inches above your spinning yo-yo, take the string between the thumb and forefinger of your yo-yo hand. Take the thumb of your non-yo-yo hand and put it through the loop.

3. Twist your hand in a *counterclockwise* direction and snag the string hanging down from the thumb and forefinger of your non-yo-yo hand with the thumb and forefinger of your yo-yo hand.

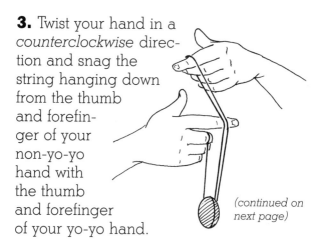

(continued on next page)

4. With your non-yo-yo hand, spread the string apart and pull down to form the bottom of the "cradle." Swing the yo-yo back and forth as you would in Rock the Baby.

5. Still holding the string, bring your non-yo-yo hand back over the yo-yo hand so that it is in the same position it was in before you made your "cradle." Pull the thumb of your non-yo-yo hand out of the long loop, let go of the string you are holding in your yo-yo hand, and flip your yo-yo back on the Trapeze.

6. Flip the yo-yo into the air and catch it to finish the trick.

EIFFEL TOWER
Level 3

This is another trick that is named very appropriately. Practice with a dead yo-yo first to get the string just right.

1. Throw down a good, fast sleeper, then slip the forefinger and thumb of your non-yo-yo hand under the string and turn them *counterclockwise*.

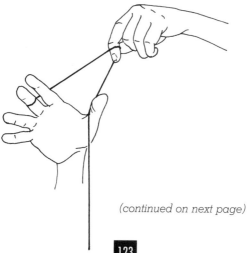

(continued on next page)

123

2. Drop your yo-yo hand and hook the string over the outside of your thumb. The string should look like an hourglass.

3. With the thumb and forefinger of your non-yo-yo hand, pinch the string to form the bottom of the tower.

4. Pull up with your non-yo-yo hand while catching the dangling string between your string finger and your ring finger.

5. To dismantle the tower, release all the string. The yo-yo will spin back into your hand.

LEVEL 4 TRICKS

SHOOT THE MOON
Level 4

When you get very comfortable with this trick, see how many continuous Shoot the Moons you can do!

1. Start off by throwing a Forward Pass (see page 70), but as the yo-yo comes toward you, toss it up by flicking your wrist.

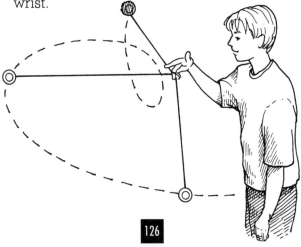

2. When the yo-yo comes about two-thirds of the way back down, give it a good, brisk forward toss. The yo-yo will go back out in front of you.

WHIRLYBIRD
Level 4

This is a two-handed trick. First practice throwing Inside Loops with both hands. When you feel comfortable doing that, alternate Inside Loops with Outside Loops.

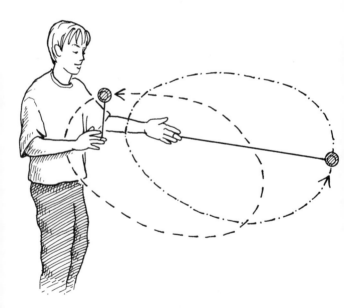

CRISSCROSS
Level 4+

This is also a two-handed yo-yo trick.

1. Begin by throwing Inside Loops with both hands.

2. Cross the strings. While one yo-yo is going out, make the other yo-yo come toward you.

3. When you want this madness to end, return the yo-yos to your hand.

LUNAR ECLIPSE
Level 4+

This is another combination trick.

1. Begin by throwing Inside Loops, and as you complete your second or third loop, go into a Shoot the Moon.

2. When the yo-yo comes back, launch two more Inside Loops.

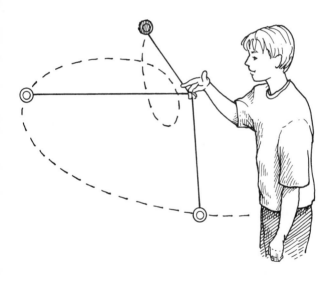

Lucky Meisenheimer—yo-yo collector supreme—shows off his collection.

CHAPTER 6

YO-YO
Collecting
and
Memorabilia

Most yoers not only play with
yo-yos but collect them.
Some have just a few, others own hundreds. Lucky
Meisenheimer of Orlando, Florida, has
the largest collection in the world, con-
sisting of more than 4,000 yo-yos and
articles of yo-yo memorabilia.

What is yo-yo memorabilia? It's
basically anything that has a picture of
a yo-yo on it. Here's just a partial list:
yo-yos, yo-yo buttons, yo-yo badges,

yo-yo plaques, yo-yo store signs and yo-yo displays, yo-yo string packages, yo-yo trick books, yo-yo display boxes, yo-yo trick sheets, yo-yo shirts, yo-yo caps, yo-yo autographs, yo-yo jackets . . .

What Kind of YO-YOs Do People Collect?

Most yo-yo collectors don't collect yo-yos as an investment. They collect because a certain yo-yo reminds them of their first one, or they feel the nostalgia an old yo-yo carries with it.

As Lucky Meisenheimer says, "Any yo-yo is collectible." If you want to collect yo-yos and you're just starting out, he recommends Spectra Star Yo-Yos. (Spectra Star is the company that makes the Star Wars, Ghostbuster, Batman, and cartoon character yo-yos.)

Here are some other famous yo-yo names you should look for: Festival,

Royal, Goody, Cheerio, Dell, Alox, Hyker, and Fli-Back. What kind of yo-yo is collectible? The answer is: the one that appeals to you.

Where Can I Find Old YO-YOs?

Your friends, family, and relatives are a good place to begin searching for old yo-yos. You'd be surprised how many closet yoers there are in the world and how many people never throw their yo-yos away. They put them in trunks and desk drawers and in attics and basements. You might find out your Aunt Agnes was a Duncan champion before she threw her back out, or maybe your Uncle Earl uses an old yo-yo to keep his desk level. Your friends might have old yo-yos handed down from their parents.

Some of the best yo-yo finds happen because you ask the right person. But if you're still a little frustrated, try flea markets, garage sales, and second-hand stores. Over *half a billion* yo-yos are out there—somewhere.

Info from Those in the Know

For years, yo-yo collectors suffered from a lack of information. Now, two esteemed yo-yo collectors have written books that explain the art of collecting yo-yos.

Lucky Meisenheimer has written **Lucky's Guide to Yo-Yo Collecting.** For information on this book, write to him at 7300 Sandlake Commons Blvd., Suite 105, Orlando, FL 32819.

Another yo-yo professional, Chris Cook, has written a book called **Collectible American Yo-Yos.** It's available from Collector Books for $16.00. For more information, call (800) 626-5420.

If you don't know much about yo-yos, these books will give you a good idea of what old yo-yos looked like.

CHAPTER 7

I Want to Know More about Yo-ing and YO-YOs

If you want to know more about becoming an expert yoer, there's loads of information if you know where to look. Here are places where you can get anything that has to do with yo-yos!

The American YO-YO Association (AYYA)

The American Yo-Yo Association is a group of collectors, manufacturers, players, both pro and amateur, and people who just love yo-yos. Members receive tips and information on yo-yo events and what's new in the hobby.

Associate Life Member: $3.00. Includes membership card, membership patch, and one issue of the AYYA news. This is a nonvoting lifetime membership, but it can be converted into an active membership at any time. To receive a year's subscription to *The Yo-Yo Times*, include an additional $10.00.

Active Life Member: $10.00 per year. With this membership, you receive a card, the patch, AYYA newsletters, and voting privileges.

Active Student Member (18 and under): $5.00 per year. Includes the items offered with the Active Life Membership. A year's subscription to *The Yo-Yo Times* costs an extra $8.00.

For more information or to ask questions, write to:

AYYA
627 163rd Street, South
Spanaway, WA 98387

YO-YO Newsletters

For up-to-date information on contests, yo-yos, and product information, here are two periodicals devoted exclusively to yo-yo players:

The Yo-Yo Times ($12.00/5 issues)
P. O. Box 1519-WB
Herndon, VA 20172
E-mail: yoyotime@aol.com

The Noble Disk
($10.00/4 issues)
132 #11 Middle Street
Portsmouth, NH 03801
(603) 427-2473

YO-YO Competitions

The best way to stay informed of yo-yo competitions, both in your area and anywhere in the country, is by subscribing to either *The Yo-Yo Times* or *The Noble Disk.* The American Yo-Yo Association's newsletter is also an excellent source for upcoming yo-yo-related events.

If you don't think you have the skills to compete but want to watch the best in action, attend a yo-yo competition. It could provide the inspiration you need to reach new heights in your yo-yo abilities. Going to these events is also a great way to meet people who want to learn how to yo or who can teach you.

YO-YO Clubs

The best way to learn yo-yo tricks is with others who are also learning. Yo-yo clubs are a great way to get started.

Many high schools and colleges have clubs. If there are none in your area, you can always start your own. Begin by advertising at your school or in your town newspaper. (Community service listings are usually free!) Advertising in *The Yo-Yo Times* or *The Noble Disk* can help, too.

Once you get a club going, you can probably find an adult who knows a few yo-yo tricks (and there are a lot of them out there!) to act as coach.

Or write to the American Yo-Yo Association for assistance. They can help you find professionals in your area. You might even get a yo-yo champ to come to your club meeting!

YO-YO Manufacturers

Every manufacturer makes their own kind of special yo-yo. As you become more skilled at yo-ing, you might want to check out some of the other types and designs of yo-yos on the market. Here's a list of the companies that make yo-yos today.

(Please refer back to this list for all addresses of yo-yo companies when sending away for videos, yo-yos, or other promotional materials listed in this chapter and the next.)

Duncan Toys
P. O. Box 97
Middlefield, OH 44062

Oliver Toys
439 Northwood Drive
S. San Francisco, CA 94080

Playmaxx
2947 East Grant Road
Tucson, AZ 85716
(520) 322-0100

Tom Kuhn Yo-Yos, Ltd.
2383 California Street
San Francisco, CA 94115
(800) 879-6967

What's Next (maker of BC Yo-Yos)
P. O. Box 276
Arcade, NY 14009
(800) 458-8635

Wooden Monarch Yo-Yos
P. O. Box 23404
Santa Barbara, CA 93121
(805) 966-4270

Yomega Corp.-YR
Retail Dept.
P. O. Box 4146
Fall River, MA 02723-0402
(800) 338-8796

YO-YO Trick Books

Yo-yo trick books have been around almost since the day Donald Duncan began producing yo-yos. They offer diagrams showing how to perform many yo-yo tricks. They are inexpensive, and many companies offer them along with their yo-yos. Here are just a few trick books available.

Duncan Yo-Yo and Spin Top Book
This booklet illustrates 35 tricks and is more than 40 pages long. It costs $2.50 and is available from Duncan.

Pumping Wood
This is a two-sided single sheet from Tom Kuhn Yo-Yos specially printed for use with the No-Jive 3-in-1 yo-yo.

The Bluebook of Yo
This book illustrates yo-yo tricks. It costs $1.50 and is available from *The Yo-Yo Times*.

Getting Ready to Yo-Yo!

This is a single sheet available from Oliver Toys. It illustrates 15 tricks, and it explains string length and other yo-yo techniques.

YO-YO Videos

If you would like to learn how to do tricks and there is no one who can teach you, yo-yo videos are an excellent substitute. Here are some available videos.

Yo for It!

This video costs $10.00 (plus $3.00 shipping and handling) and is available from Oliver Toys.

Yo! The Video Show

This video shows how to perform more than 60 tricks. It costs $20.00 and includes an Imperial Yo-Yo and a pack of yo-yo strings. The package is available from the Duncan Toy Company.

Duncan How to Yo-Yo (#3110VE)

Duncan professional Arne Dixon demonstrates 60 yo-yo tricks. This video also covers yo-yo collecting and history. It costs $10.00 and is available from Duncan.

Yomega Power Spin Yo-Yo Video

This video shows how to perform yo-yo tricks. It costs $14.95 (plus $3.50 shipping and handling). You can get the video plus a Yomega yo-yo for $19.95 (plus $3.50 shipping and handling). The video and the video/yo-yo package are available from Yomega Corp.

The Vid-e-Yo

This is an hour-long "how-to" tape. It costs $19.95, and it's available from Playmaxx.

It's Yo-Yo Time

This video is put out by *The Yo-Yo Times*. It costs $19.95 (plus $2.50 shipping and handling). (Note that the P. O. Box is slightly different from the one listed on page 141. For this particular offer, it's P. O. Box 1519-YTT.)

McBride's String Trick Video
This video costs $10.00 (plus $3.00 shipping and handling) and is available from Tom Kuhn Yo-Yos, Ltd.

Following are yo-yo videos that are no longer being produced. But if you ever have a chance to see one, yo for it!

Smothers Brothers Yo-Yo Man Video
Tom Smothers is the universal yo-yo ambassador. This video was made a few years ago, and many libraries lend it. There is a chance you can still buy one by sending $12.95 (plus $3.00 shipping and handling) to:

Smothers Brothers
Yo-Yo Man Video
P. O. Box 789
Kenwood, CA 95452

Yo-Yo Man (1978)

This is a documentary video about one of the original Filipino demonstrators of the Duncan yo-yo, Nemo Concepción. It was shot for the Smithsonian Festival of American Folk Life when Nemo was 77 years of age. This is difficult to find, but your local library may have a copy for rental.

The best way to learn about yo-yos is with others.

YO-YO Supplies

Transaxle Lubrication

Made especially for transaxle yo-yos, Yomega Brain Lube comes with a lubricating pen. It is nontoxic and costs $3.29. It's available from the Yomega Corp.

YO-YO Pouches

Get your yo-yo out of your pocket and into a specially made pouch that can be worn on your belt.

The Yomega Leather Yo-Yo Belt Pouch costs $6.00 and is available from the Yomega Corp.

Tom Kuhn's Leather Belt Pouch for Yo-Yos costs $8.00 and is available from Tom Kuhn Yo-Yos, Ltd.

Playmaxx Yolster (#1500) costs only $1.00 and is available from Playmaxx.

CHAPTER 8

YO-YO Miscellany

YO-YO Museums

Some people realized a long time ago that yo-yos were something special to be treasured and displayed. Here are two excellent museums that display a wide range of fascinating yo-yos from the 1920s to the present.

The National Yo-Yo Museum
320 Broadway
Chico, CA 95926
(916) 893-0545

The Yozeum, home to some of the world's most interesting yo-yos and memorabilia.

The Yozeum
2900 N. Country Club
Tucson, AZ 85716
(520) 322-0100

YO-YOs on the Internet

If you have access to a computer and the Internet, here are some excellent sources of information.

The American Yo-Yo Association
http://www.pd.net/yoyo

Cosmics Yo-Yo Trick Page
cosmicfr@inlink.com

Playmaxx
www.playmaxx.com

Duncan Home Page
http://www.kidshoponline.com/
duncan/index.html

E-mail Addresses

General E-mail questions and information can be found on the following website dedicated to the yo-yo:
socoolbob@socool.com

Oliver Toys
yopro@aol.com

Wooden Monarch Yo-Yos
mreid@rain.org

YO-YO Records

Here are some amazing records held by some of the top professional yo-yo players in the world.

Longest Spinner: Dale Oliver. Using a Playmaxx Pro-Yo, Dale got the Pro-Yo to spin for an incredible 51 seconds.

Fastest Spinner: Dale Oliver. Using a Playmaxx Pro-Yo, Dale got his yo-yo to spin 14,400 times in a minute.

Around the Worlds: From one spin, Dale Oliver got his Pro-Yo to go Around the World 26 times. (Using a transaxle SB-2, he got it to go Around the World 102 times.)

Dale Oliver: 1995 YO-YO World Champion

Dale got the yo-yo bug when he was only 12 years old. By the time he was 15, Dale had won some money and many prizes. He was then recruited by Duncan yo-yo legend Wayne Lundberg to work as a demonstrator.

Dale left school when he was 17 to work full-time (which meant lots of traveling) for Duncan. He left Duncan in 1963 to devote time to his own projects.

By the 1970s, Dale was working for

Duncan's successor, Flambeau. He left Flambeau in 1974 and went to work with Donald F. Duncan Jr. at Playmaxx. He left in 1978, but not before he decided to design his own line of yo-yos.

Today, Dale can perform more than 200 yo-yo tricks with deceptive ease. In 1995 he founded Oliver Toys, which now produces the Terminator and the Terminator Tornado Ball-Bearing yo-yos.

In October 1993 Dale founded the American Yo-Yo Association. These days, he is busy teaching new yo-yo enthusiasts the science of yo-ing. He tours schools all over the country, using the yo-yo to demonstrate the science and physics of yo-yos. His course is called "Yo-Yo Fun and the Science of Spin."

Tom Kuhn: YO-YO Innovator

Tom Kuhn had a problem. He couldn't find a wooden yo-yo that didn't

Tom Kuhn

fall apart. His wife gave him a nice wooden one, but after a short while it broke! So Tom did what any frustrated yo-yo entrepreneur would do: he started tinkering with his own wooden creations. Now, twenty years later, his company makes some of the most sought-after yo-yos in the business.

In his early years, Tom got to be a pretty good yoer. He once won a prized rhinestone-studded Duncan yo-yo at a competition. But in the late '70s, most of the yo-yos in the stores were plastic, and Tom didn't like them.

After years of work and thousands of tries, he perfected his first wooden yo-yo. At first, he gave them to friends and avid yoers or he sold them at flea markets. But soon, word of mouth brought eager customers to him!

Now Tom's yo-yos are big business and that keeps him busy. But he keeps even busier with his day job—he's a dentist!

Brad Countryman

Brad designs and sells his own line of popular yo-yos. He calls his company "What's Next?" and many yoers all over the world wonder what his next beautiful yo-yo creation will be. He makes his yo-yos out of traditional rock maple, then creates colorful and unique designs, which he laminates onto the wood. His are some of the most eye-pleasing and comfortable yo-yos anywhere.

Brad Countryman

Donald F. Duncan Jr.

Donald Duncan Jr. continues his father's legacy as a manufacturer in the yo-yo business. Like millions of other children, the yo-yo left a lasting impression on him, and when his father's company was taken over by Flambeau, he went out on his own. Three times he tried and failed to set up a business in which he could license and manufacture his own yo-yo.

Finally, in January 1988, Donald opened up his own yo-yo business. His company is called Playmaxx and they manufacture three kinds of fixed-axle yo-yos. Dale Oliver used a Playmaxx yo-yo to set up his record for longest non-transaxle spinner!

Donald stresses that yo-yos should no longer be considered "just toys." Now that yo-yos are so popular all over the world, he would like to see them added to the Olympics someday.

YO-YO Facts and Trivia

• The World's Most Valuable Yo-Yo belonged to country star Roy Acuff. The yo-yo was a present from Acuff to President Richard Nixon. Nixon tried a few yo-yo tricks with it (he didn't fare very well), then autographed the yo-yo and gave it back to Acuff. When Acuff died, the yo-yo was sold at auction. It fetched $16,000.

• According to the Duncan Yo-Yo Company, yo-yos are the world's second-oldest known toy. The oldest? The doll.

• In Germany a yo-yo was called a *coblentz*.

• Of all the former presidents, the best yo-yoer was John F. Kennedy. Richard Nixon and Lyndon Johnson were also yo-yo players.

• Since the 1930s, over half a billion yo-yos have been made and sold.

• Yo-yos are very popular now in Japan, Australia, New Zealand, Israel, England, Canada, and South America.

• Donald F. Duncan Jr., son of Duncan Yo-Yo founder Donald F. Duncan, is trying to get yo-yo-ing entered as an Olympic sport.

• The first World Yo-Yo contest was held in 1932.

• Donald Duncan paid Pedro Flores $25,000 to buy Flores's yo-yo company. It was the best $25,000 he ever spent!

• The Osmond Brothers had a hit on their hands when they recorded "Yo-Yo" back in the 1970s. Maybe, like a yo-yo, it will come back.

• Tom Kuhn owns the world's largest wooden yo-yo. It's called The Bird in Hand, and it measures 50 inches by 31½ inches. It weighs 256 pounds. To get it to go, it is dropped from an 80-foot crane. And it works!

• In July 1992, astronaut Jeffrey Hoffman tried out a Tom Kuhn SB-2 on the space shuttle *Atlantis*. It went around the world 127 times and traveled 3,321,007 miles.

YO-YO TRICK INDEX

YO-YO
PHOTOGRAPHY CREDITS